Crowns

ALSO BY GAIL FISHMAN GERWIN

Sugar and Sand
Dear Kinfolk,

Crowns

Poems by

Gail Fishman Gerwin

Kelsay Books

Cover art: Hadassa Zusman

Library of Congress Control Number: 2015955478

ISBN 13: 978-0692555620

Kelsay Books
Aldrich Press
24600 Mountain Avenue 35
Hemet, California 92544

*Always for my family—
those who are here,
those in my heart*

Acknowledgments

Grateful acknowledgment is made to the following journals and sites where poetry in this collection appears:

Adanna: "Morning" and "Night Flyer"

Edison Literary Review: "First Love"

Exit 13: "Hope" (as "Budapest, 1983"), "Pelicans at Sunrise," and "To My Lost Town"

Eye to the Telescope: After *"Origins III, High Contrast Karma"* (as "Orbs")

First Literary Review-East: "Ambush"

Ithaca Lit: "Believe Me" and "Terror"

Jewish Women's Literary Annual: "It's All There," "Pants, Reborn," and "What I Don't Know"

Journal of New Jersey Poets: "Afloat," "Cats of Whitehead Street" (as "Dropping Names"), "Gifts," and "The Tablecloth"

Lips: "Business as Usual," "Life Music," "Miss Glick," "Sixteen, Candles Extinguished," and "Why I Can't Part with Fisher-Price People"

Loch Raven Review: "Dressed for Life" and "Roll 'em"

Paterson Literary Review: "A State In Mind," "Crowns," and "My Skype Cousin"

Ragazine: "Slick: a Love Story," "Time," and "Vapor"

Raritan Valley Library Anthology: "Mrs. Piggle-Wiggle"

Schuylkill Valley Journal: "The Pose"

Shot Glass Journal: "Clothes for the Holidays," "My Sea," "The Sun Will Rise Between Gaza and Raflach," and "Yom Asai, Yom Basal (A Day of Honey, A Day of Onion)"

The Red Wheelbarrow: "Dear Ben" and "Nom de Plume"

The Stillwater Review: "Shadows" (as "Budapest Shadows, 1983")

U.S. 1 Worksheets: "A Proper Gentleman," "Quiet," and "Where are the Hens?"

Verse-Virtual: "Happy Day," "Here," "Love in Geary," "My Doctors," and "Parking 101"

Contents

Epilogue: Crowns
About the Author

Foreword

Why *Crowns*?

Touring the Tower of London thirty years ago with our teenage daughters, we saw the Crown Jewels. As we followed the path around protective cases, awed by the spectrum of gems—3,000 in King George's 1937 coronation crown alone, an alarm suddenly blared from speakers, and iron gates came down to prevent exit. It truly terrified us. How to protect our children? After a while, the gates lifted; lightening had struck the Tower in a flash storm and set off the warning blasts. We were ready to leave the crowns and other treasures, happy to catalog this experience as a memory.

The crowns in this volume are memories I carry within. Stories of my ancestors, the miraculous moon rock I saw before I gave birth for the first time, young men and women who entered and left my life, kinfolk who are gone, kinfolk who remain, and the growing grandchildren—jewels who add sunshine to my days.

Special thanks to family, friends, and colleagues in poetry who continue to provide the support that fosters the words I write.

*The crown of life is neither happiness
nor annihilation; it is understanding.*
—Winifred Holtby

Prologue: Nom de Plume?

They teased me unmercifully, kids in school,
campers of my summers. Not about the way
I walked, talked, not about my girth or lack

of worth, not about my hair, sporting the neck
point of a '50s D.A. From the first day I stepped
into kindergarten, they teased me about my name,

something I couldn't change, the name that evoked
oceans over craggy reefs, schools of striped swimmers.
They made up songs, *I'm Fishing for a White Christmas,*

When You Fish Upon a Star. They asked to see my gills,
my fins, held their noses when they passed me in the halls,
pretended to faint from the odor. They blew fishface bubbles,

mwah mwah mwah, moved their rears side to side, plied fake
waters. When I spurned a dark-haired suitor near the summer
lake, his redfaced twin brother led a chorus to chant *Let us*

do the rhumba, the Fishy Fishman Rhumba. My albatross,
emblazoned on the sides of my father's moving vans, rumbling
through the streets of Paterson, headed for outlying towns,

down to Florida, up to Maine, carrying my shame for what's
in a name. After I married (imagine, a Pisces!), I made his name
mine as I traveled the road to seniority. Yet when my parents

were no more, I thought more fondly of the F-word—Fishman,
the name of my father, his father, a winter wrap to warm me
like the skin over my bones, and I began to use it on my works,

my signatures, my life, as I danced the *Fishy Fishman Rhumba*,
box-steps, one-sweep-three-four one-sweep-three-four, to release
my song—*Fishman Fishman Fishman.*

Time

We plan

As we planned our trip to Prague, we said we would take a
train to Plauen, the Saxon town where you lived, birthed seven
children, my mother the youngest. Your sepia photo, arm on
your husband's shoulder, bears the address Bahnhofstrasse 19,
next to the hotel we'd booked. The town clerk's email: *be sure
to visit the lace museum.* I still own the lace my grandfather
tatted in this town. I drape it on my shoulders, try to sense his
fingers working the loops. Once in Prague we knew the trip
was too long, too many transfers, a driver too costly. *Someday
we'll go to Berlin*, we told each other, *from there we'll take a
direct train, we have time, we have time.*

our lives

On my fourth anniversary my mother gave me your gold
bracelet with red and green stones, *give it to your youngest
daughter on her fourth anniversary,* she said, *my mother
gave it to me when your father and I were married four
years. Carry on the tradition, tell your daughter to do
the same.* My younger daughter birthed sons.

with devotion

On Fridays at sundown, I kindle candles in your silver
candlesticks, 1862 etched in the base. Were they your
own mother's? Did candles burn in your Plauen home?

and full hearts,

You may have called *Gin* when you died playing cards with
my sister the year before I was born. Perhaps you put down
the Queen of Hearts before your own heart stopped.

waiting.

Plauen, my mother's birthplace, your home, her history.
Do we have time?

They Were

Augusta, Nana

In the photo you look serene, not yet
pulled down by your husband's dreams,
his skill for tatting lace left behind
in Germany when you sailed.

My sister watched you fall still as you played
Gin with her. It was your death that gave me
your name.

You died before you could know that your
beloved son with his gentle air, your cherished
daughter with her raven hair, were slaughtered
simply because they were.

In the photo you look serene, undaunted by hard
journeys, unscathed by sad truths, unmarred by
cracks in the paper, cracks that form a mosaic
of your face.

Now older than you were at death, I look in the
mirror, see your nose, your soft lips, your dark
eyes, but Nana, I can't seize the spirit that makes
you look serene.

Saul, Papa

When the 1920 census-takers visited you
on Lexington Avenue, you told them you
were Polish. What? My mother told me you
lived in Germany, she spoke German, sang
to my children in German.

Email: *it is possible to access birth records*
in Poland, records that travel back a century,
even more. The records from Poland—suddenly
there for me to tap.

I search the index, so many provinces, so many towns.
No success until I punch in Kielce, Gubernia, keyboard
your name and there! It pops up, your birth record: Saul
Aron, with the surname my cousin Susan said you owned
before you changed it in New York. Born in 1857,
youngest of six, to Pinkus and Edjla.

My grandfather Saul, infant boy in a line of ancestors,
a line that stretches back. How far? Where did your
sisters, your brother Samuel settle? I own a photo
of us, your hands on my three-year-old shoulders.
I don't remember you now.

Saul Aron Stecki, lacemaker, poet, a lettered line in an
index of far-off names, a line that created your wealth
of children with Augusta, five who escaped the fiery fate
of their siblings. Saul Aron Stecki, a skipping stone in a
stream that flowed across the Atlantic.

My Skype Cousin

You have a cousin Hadassa, my mother Cele
said to my young self, *she lives in Israel, her
mother and I share the same name* (really Zilly).
I recall boxes of clothing Mama packed, took to
the downtown post office, sent across the sea to
the family she'd never met save for letters on sheer
blue paper. The rest of that family? My mother's
sister, brother, their spouses: snatched from their
homes, herded to a ghetto, carted to the camps.

     Eliminated.

One box bound for Israel held my sister's blue tulle
prom gown, strapless. The gown became Hadassa's
wedding dress, demure bodice and illusion veil sewn
from the underskirt. In the photo Zilly mailed, Hadassa,
only twenty, resembles my mother—apple-cheeked,
glimmer of mischief in her eyes.

With our young daughters, we traveled to Israel in 1979,
a tour with a troop of teachers, the price was right. For
months before, we tried to locate these cousins, wrote to the
Red Cross, other agencies. No letters reached Israel, a postal
strike. *Your father wanted to go to Israel,* my mother said,
I was afraid to fly, I would have met Zilly. After my father
died, Mama would not go, not alone, not with a widow's
group, not with us, *I couldn't do that to your father.*

Facebook. I find a woman with the same last name as my
cousin's family, her profile photo atop a horse (my family?
on a horse?), message her privately. *No,* she writes, *I don't
know of anyone by that name in the city you mention,* though

weeks later she messages me—*here's an address, maybe you should write*. I send a letter (no postal strike), include my email address. It reaches Hadassa's brother, a cousin born long after the war, a cousin with the same September birth date as my daughter.

He friends me on Facebook (*look, a photo of my little girl*), then gives me his sister's email address. Hadassa! I write, she writes, I send her poetry, she sends me artwork, tells me her mother died years before our long-ago trip. (My mother would not have met her.)

Skype. We connect, touch our screens, the closest we might ever come to holding hands. We cry, we giggle. She tells me her story, how she and her mother slipped from the ghetto (*a woman gave us her papers*), wandered through the seasons for four years, slept in rail stations, other shelters, hid from demons who took her aunts, uncles, grandmother, grandfather.

Her baby sister Juliane.

All we ate were potato skins, all we owned were the clothes on our backs, she says, *someone even stole my mother's underpants in winter from the hook where they were drying, We hid in a Dresden church while bombs fell, then made our way to Israel.*

She and her iPad take me on a tour of her apartment high above the Mediterranean. From my chair in New Jersey, I revisit the sea where my daughters did cartwheels in a town minutes away from where she lived, where I

couldn't find her. Behind her a Tiffany lamp she crafted.
Eggs sizzle on her cooktop, salad awaits in a glass bowl.
I introduce her to my husband, show her our dog.

Technology takes us across miles and years that separate us,
lets us share our aging faces, lets us learn about each other
as we never could when my mother told me—*you have*
a cousin Hadassa, she lives in Israel, her mother and I
share the same name.

Art across the Atlantic

Cousin Hadassa
Sends me art from her iPad
Write the words, she says

Yom Asai, Yom Basal (A Day of Honey, A Day of Onion)
    Tears of peeled onion
    Burn, await the taste, the balm
    Of honey on tongue

My Sea
    Today it seems at peace
    But deception hides in the
    Breakers, the silence broken

The Sun Will Rise Between Gaza and Raflach
    Girls atop their tanks
    Spread flowers around poised guns
    Peace, they sing, *see? Peace*

Clothes for the Holidays
    On the boulevard
    We strut, gossip, share our wish
    Next year, Jerusalem

Here
    It's here that we sit
    It's here we find each other
    Here: you touch my soul

My Doctors
    I see their brain cells
    Through the fog of discussion
    Heal me, cure me now

Love in Geary
Twined together in
A dream worth its golden weight
Two should live as one

Happy Day
Rejoice, we are alive
See? Our loved ones call our names
Come, let's dance, let's sing

A State in Mind

My cousin Susan lives in Santa Fe, where green
chile is a household staple that sets your head afire.
My cousin Susan, so jovial, so ready to arrange
others' lives that I named her Bossy, *clean out
those cabinets,* she tells me, *take photos, send
them to me, prove you can do it.*

I don't know how she places her right foot in front
of her left, not because she's had two hips and both
knees replaced, but because she endured the worst
day ever, the day the call came from Japan, *your
son,* someone probably told her, *your son on a bike,
a car hit him.*

Shiva over, my cousin Susan sold her Detroit
home, her husband Maurice sold his business,
they moved to Santa Fe, where they could see
the Sandia range where Josh skied, where they
could take shelter under the neon blue sky
that holds unfettered sun. Santa Fe, adobe
icon of the state that called their son to college,
the state where he flourished, the state he
would not see again.

She tells me: *I was a zombie, I walked through
Walmart for two years without purpose, held
on to the cart so I wouldn't collapse.* She sat
in the town plaza, befriended the homeless.
Maurice found a studio, filled canvases with
color, molded clay into humans.

My cousin Susan lives in a home they built
where the patio peers at the Sandias. *A crow
led us to the lot*, she says, *was that crow Josh?*

Maurice sculpts and paints Billy the Kid, his
replicas of this notorious legend and cohorts
now the center of a permanent exhibit. *Look*,
someone says at the dedication where family
and friends from around the country gather,
I see Josh in the Kid's gaze.

My cousin Susan lives in Santa Fe,
where green chile sets her pain afire.

Dear Ben,

Letters to Daddy. Tucked in your file cabinet in the corner
of my basement. I climb over an old sofa, storage boxes,
curio cabinets that didn't sell on Craigslist. Then I find them.

Superstorm Sandy: giant oaks shudder, list but stand, only
the Internet is gone. *You're lucky*, says Stephanie from
Cablevision, *you're lucky to be alive*. I feel lucky—I hold
your romance on paper in my hands. *Dear Ben*, they all
begin, *Dear Ben*, on fragile bond. You're in Detroit, you're
in upstate New York, you're everywhere but with him.

*Dear Ben, thank you for the purse but where's my fruit
candy? Dear Ben, thank you for the dress, I'm dying for
some ice cream, please mail me some, ha ha. Dear Ben,
I'm coming back in June, well in time for my birthday
present, oh, can you send me stockings? If you don't
trust me, send them C.O.D.*

Dear Ben, will you buy me a flivver?

So that's what the photo shows—a flivver. Where is it?
There you perch on the hood. Four friends surround you,
your round cheeks puffed in a smile, your thumb at play atop
a crony's curls. She's in knickers, your legs hidden though I'm
sure you wear shoes, maybe those you asked for. (*Dear Ben,
remember, I wear a five and a half.*) Did you drive? You spent
your married life as a passenger. Where did your moxie go?

Dear Ben, I send loads of love, Dear Ben, meet me at a hundred twenty-ninth street, the boat from Kingston arrives at six in the morning. Dear Ben, those letters from Sam mean nothing to me, you shouldn't worry, so only half a kiss this time.

My dearest Ben, I saw a dandy picture yesterday, it's called Three Weeks. Ben, my love, I quit my job. I'll be home soon.

Dear Ben, will you buy me a flivver?

Gifts

My Aunt Helen, sixth in the crop of seven
born to my grandmother in Plauen, could not
spell. Every post card, every birthday greeting,
our wedding check—all added a *Y* to the middle
of the name my parents gave me at birth. When
corrected, she'd say *oh yes, I know*, then proceed
to gift me with that *Y* until the April day she died,
and we drove up to Paterson to tell her baby sister,
my mother, the sad news.

Aunt Helen, generous with the alphabet,
generous with her keepsakes, gifted me:
a necklace I rarely remove, a bracelet, its
etched roses a thornless circle that rounds
my wrist, a curio cabinet that holds my
grandfather's spectacles and my mother's
Limoges candy dish that stored M&Ms.

Aunt Helen, whose spelling began in German,
Yiddish, whose life was touched by trauma—
twin sons who died within her, a daughter
who remained a non-reader, a non-speller.

She gifted me again, again, as I watched her
dive from unspeakable heights into backyard
pools in upstate New York, as I danced with her
in shoe departments when she snatched my arm,
twirled me to piped-in Muzak tunes from *the old
days*. And now? On the final day of the Festival
of Booths, when we gather to remember the dead,
I recall Aunt Helen, who danced through the alphabet
to gift me with an extra letter.

Pants, Reborn

The first hint my mother felt of the rebirth of my father's
brown pleated pants was when Schwartz the cleaner

delivered them in protective blue plastic to the front door
on Wednesday, five days after she'd thrown them in the trash

for pickup. *It's time*, she'd told Daddy, *look how they shine,
I can see my reflection in the thighs, and oh, those shredded,*

cuffs, you can't call on customers in them. Yet there they were,
cuffs, reflective fabric, cleaned, pressed, perfect creases up the leg

fronts. *Ben,* she said, *what are they doing here, I threw them away,
you saw me.* The man who'd moved his family from a changing

neighborhood to a street in a new school district, the man who'd
built a ranch home with the money he'd earned after a lifetime

of carrying others' furniture across town, across the country,
the man whose sepia photo as a teen in knickers with his

immigrant father in front of a beaten-down house on Tyler Street
near the Passaic River hangs on a wall in my home—the man who

could afford a new pair of slacks, showed her where Schwartz,
who'd perhaps learned his craft from his own immigrant father in

an Eleventh Avenue storefront, had rehemmed threadbare cuffs,
had made the pants new again, *look how they shine*, Daddy said,

before he took the hanger, strode down the hall to their bedroom,
hung them in his closet to join other slacks, to wait for tomorrow.

Emeralds

When I was eighteen, my parents gave me a ring.
They'd gone downtown to Paterson's Church Street,
a street that had seen its glory days when the Silk City
was a destination, not a town where its children couldn't
leave fast enough. The jeweler Frank Slugh worked
in a third-floor loft, the paned window sealed shut.

The ring: platinum with pavé diamonds in a sideways
oval. Two triangles within the gem path held emeralds,
my May birthstone. I wore the ring on the fourth finger
of my left hand, where someday a single diamond was
meant to rest (a sign that someone loved me). I relished
this ring of freedom, it marked my years—eighteen—old
enough to order a Tom Collins in Suffern, across the border
in New York (my cousin Seymour drove me), old enough
to study in ivied halls where the Parthenon glittered (if only
in texts), where Lady Chatterley frolicked, where I could
learn to teach.

When that someone finally found me—much later than my
fretful family hoped, the ring moved to my right hand, made
way for the solitaire that sent me along paths of marriage,
motherhood, far from home, from my parents, from eighteen,
when so much seemed possible.

I cannot give the ring to one of my daughters,
I cannot give the ring to my granddaughter,
I cannot find the ring where deep green jewels,
like two eyes that could see the future,
                    beckoned me.

Quick, Hide!

American Doctor with Ebola
Arrives in U.S. for Treatment
—*The New York Times,* August 2, 2014

It isn't just for West Africa, cautions the media,
virus here in our back yard. Facebook comments:
how dare they bring someone back for treatment,
how could they let him walk free, wasn't he supposed
to be in a protective tube?

My mom and dad hid me when polio drove my afflicted
generation to archaic vessels, iron lungs. They hid me
with other children from Paterson in summer camp—fresh
air, fresh kids, still alive, able to walk, play softball, sing
about the glory of the lake and surrounding pines, parental
visits from New Jersey's cities of disease confined to a field
across the road while we wept for the comfort of their arms.

First Love

When I was fifteen, I was a counselor-in-training at Camp
Lincoln-Laurel, a rustic enclave near Blairstown, long after
the polio epidemic drove parents to hide us in summer camps
where the paralyzing disease might not find us, long before

vaccines saved my children, their children. That summer
I found love with Tall Richie from Manhattan, who lived on
Riverside Drive in a flatiron-shaped apartment house. Richie,
a good smoocher, enrolled at Syracuse for the fall. We'd neck

in the gazebo across from the dining room, the room where
campers sang *Gail and Richie sitting in a tree, K-I-S-S-I-N-G.*
We parted in August after one last kiss in the cooling air. Two
months later, when he asked me up for a fraternity weekend

(he'd enclosed a photo of himself in his ROTC uniform in the
letter), I planned my wardrobe and announced to my parents
where I was headed the next month. *I know the bus schedule,*
I told them, *Richie will meet me, I'll stay in the girls' dorm, see*

what he wrote? My father, not one for confrontation, slid from the
room, turned on the television, picked up the newspaper, said *Cele,
you take care of this.* Oh, she did. She told me about the kind of
girls who went for college weekends, said *the whole town talks*

about those girls, she wouldn't have me join *that* sorority. I didn't
go to Syracuse. I unfolded my saved outfits, hung them back in the
closet, never saw Richie again, yet whenever I drive along the
West Side Highway, I spot his corner apartment, my heart heavy.

Night Flyer

Above us, stars. Beneath us, constellations . . .
—Ted Kooser, "Flying at Night"

My first flight from the old Newark Airport
in an Eastern Airlines plane with four propellers
launched me toward my parents, already in
Miami Beach, maybe dancing the cha-cha
in the hotel lobby, maybe dining at Cooper's
Roumanian Restaurant, where skirt steaks
drooped over dinner-plate rims, where chopped
liver came with crispy morsels of chicken fat,
charred onions, not a statin in sight.

They'd driven south from Paterson days before,
school still in session, left me with Dotty, the
next-door neighbor, and Elinor, who trailed me
in age by a year. Two blizzards came that March
week but Dotty's freezer promised pierogies
from the new Food Fair on Madison Avenue.

Dotty's husband Jack was in the hospital, a mild
heart attack, spurring her—she'd told my parents
I'd be good company for Ellie—to put on snowshoes,
tromp a dozen blocks to visit him while Ellie and I,
on a sudden snow vacation, shared girl time, listened
to records, foraged for freezer fare.

The night after the second blizzard, more snow
in the air, Dotty drove me to Newark for my night
flight. The porter took my blue Amelia Earhart
suitcase, and I climbed tarmac stairs toward the sky,
no jetway to shield me from the chill.

Finally aloft, though I couldn't see heavenly bodies
(snow again), only fire from the propellers, which
I pointed out to the stewardess. *No danger*, she said,
normal, and I sat back, ready for adventure, not aware
that the arms awaiting me at the Miami airport wouldn't
be there forever, that my friend Ellie would die too soon
after we'd renewed our friendship in the shadow of our
senior years, that the propeller's flame would return
only in the bright softness of my memories.

Sixteen, Candles Extinguished

At the Casa Mana in Teaneck, New Jersey, we gathered to celebrate Sweet Sixteen. My dress? Strapless white eyelet, with amber velvet bows threaded along the bodice. A dozen of my best friends and their dates. My cousin Philip with a girl named Sue. Barbara, whose dad owned D'Arnold's on Broadway (they called them beauty parlors) where my hair was shorn in the popular D.A. style, brought white-shoed Jack, one of the few Jewish redheads in Paterson. We fixed up my young next-door neighbor Ellie with Eddie G., maybe because their names were similar, maybe because I wanted my second-grade boyfriend in my high school life even though I'd been sent home by his mother back then because I tested a new word—*obnoxious*—on his uncle. Paula and her date Marty wore half-pouts. Paula's ponderous twin Peter stood silent, his arm around smiling Joan's waist. Tall Marcia came with sleepy-eyed Alvin, sexy before we knew what sexy meant. Sheila brought platonic Andy and the other Joan showed off Jerry (Marty? Artie?). A fraternity boy like all the rest. And sweet Ruthie, in a scoop-neck floral dress and pearl choker, chose Steven. (Their last names rhymed.) My date? Eddie Y., who wore a wetted pompadour long before gel came on the market. Eddie, whose nose sported a wide bump, perhaps from an errant baseball. Eddie, who'd never asked me out, Eddie, who never asked me out after that. Ruthie? Long gone. Barbara? Gone. Both Joans? Gone. Little Ellie? Gone. The white eyelet dress with amber bows threaded across the bodice? Gone.

Sixteen. Sweet. Gone

Business as Usual

Paterson's phone numbers began with
words: Sherwood, Lambert, Mulberry.
In our new house, Lambert 5-2336 took
personal calls, Sherwood 2-3583 demanded
complete silence as we ate burgers broiled
in the toaster-oven on the red Formica
countertop. The Sherwood number was
an extension from the daytime office
where my mother booked jobs for my
dad's moving company.

When Sherwood 2 rang, my mother's eyes
narrowed, *be quiet*, they warned us, *this
means money for your clothes, maybe for
college, not that expensive one, you can
go to the one in the next town, you'll be
a teacher, forget this veterinarian dream,
do you want to stand under cows for the
rest of your life?*

I learned how to answer in my Sherwood
voice, to tell the person on the other end
of the wire that local would cost sixteen
dollars an hour for a van and three men,
long distance was by weight. I once took
a message but couldn't hear the last name.
*Can you repeat that? What? Can you spell it?
Oh, S-M-I-T-H. I'll have the secretary call
you in the morning to set up an estimate.*

I loved the green Lambert 5 phone.
I hated the yellow Sherwood 2 phone.
The first one meant friends, parties,
dances, homework help. The second
spelled cold dinners and parents who
seemed to care more about their business
than mine.

For Izzy

He lived across the street from us in what was called
The Mansion, a Tudor-beamed half circle that stretched
across a city block. Rumor was that they handed out dollar
bills for Halloween. He lived with his mother Anna, a redhead
from The Old Country, who walked Ike, her Weimaraner,
a friendly grey fellow with green eyes. She'd say, her words
heavy with her birth, *Ike, clean yourself out*, and—good dog,
he did. Good dog until he jumped on her with the joy of being,
knocked out her front tooth. He lived across the street, his
daughters came on weekends from their mother's home near
the park. His tennis court was open to all, *come play, bring
friends,* he'd say, *it shouldn't sit empty.* I played tennis, leapt
from his yard's playground swings into open air, landed square
on my feet, my mother furious at chances I took.

In May lilacs bloomed
Filled the air with perfume
Summer's promise

He lived across the street, walked over on summer evenings,
strode through our unlocked screen door. *Cele,* he'd say to my
mother, *what's to eat*, then open the fridge, surf her bounty.
He'd pass humid hours on our front porch, tell gathered neighbors
about silks his company wove in one of the Carolinas, far from
our town, once a city that flowed with fabric. Our home soon
sold, my parents soon gone, summer chatter a clattering memory.

In May lilacs bloom
Seclude the razed acreage
Fill the street with sweetness

Joe

After *Aristotle Contemplating a Bust of Homer*
—Rembrandt van Rijn, 1653

The Senior Mirror photo shows me in a demure
white blouse. We called them man shirts, wore
them to school with tight mid-calf skirts, on
weekends over rolled-up Levis. On my feet—
thick ribbed socks, white buck Oxfords. (We all
owned them, carried powder puffs to dab scuffs.)

Next to me on the bio lab table rests my partner,
a disembodied skull. My youth frozen in black
and white, I contemplate the head, pretend to
interview this ossified friend for the photographer.

I drag out the yearbook for a class reunion, see
the photo, think of Joe—my teacher, my mentor.
Joe, who fought for an extra year of biology for
eager students, Joe, whose lifelong illness rendered
him sightless, Joe, who—in his blindness—guided
us in dissection, discussion, his wisdom indelible
as measured brushstrokes.

He'd tell me *è buono—it is good*, his smile a beacon
as I tried to converse in Italian. Joe knighted me,
dubbed me his assistant—*you'll be my eyes*—a year
before this photo was taken, a photo he never could see.

Life Music

The worst moment of my college life
was when Charles told me we were
finished, his mother had won.

Was it because I couldn't eat her stuffed
cabbage, ugh, so sweet, not like my own
mother's with a touch of vinegar that
made the tongue curl with delight?
Was it because I couldn't converse with
his father, a scientist who sat at the table's
head, silent, glum, his brain awash with
formulas for the pickled-herring company
where he worked? What could I say to him?
I hated herring.

The best moment with Charles comes to me
whenever I hear the song "Gigi" on Broadway
radio. No, Charles didn't resemble Louis
Jourdan, not even close, but he'd taken me
to see the film on the first crisp October night.
I wore my blue and brown checked wool dress
from the seventh floor of Saks, brown Fenton
pumps from the fourth-floor shoe department.

We arrived back on campus before curfew,
before the mob scene in the dorm front hall,
couples kissing, kissing as if it were the last
time, as if the boys from Hopkins were headed
for war. We stood alone on the knoll outside,
our silhouettes outlined by a full moon, stars
like spotlights meant for us alone. He removed
his fraternity pin, told me he loved me, pinned it
over my heart.

When I told my mother on the phone the next day,
she asked me if I loved him more than I loved her
and my father. I did but didn't say the words aloud.

Don't let my mother see the pin, Charles said as we
drove up the hill to his Montclair home on Stuffed
Cabbage Night. *She won't be happy, I'm supposed to
marry the daughter of college graduates, professionals.*
My own parents, born in Europe, were immigrants, lucky
to be here, lucky they didn't remain where their relatives
were slaughtered simply for being who they were, for their
dark hair, their brown eyes, their promise.

His mother won, he let me know the following February,
I'll give you back your Goucher beer mug, he said, a smile
of triumph across his face, *I'm going to date Judy, she's
a rabbi's daughter.*

Today, as I drove up one of New Jersey's busy highways,
a poet, wife, mother, grandmother of those I celebrate
every day, there he was, Louis Jourdan on Broadway
radio, trying to crack my heart.

Terror

I'm late! I'm Late!
For a very important date . . .
—White Rabbit, *Alice in Wonderland*

She resembled one of those masks where
black-rimmed spectacles attach to a nose.
Her own nose cast its shadow over the soft
spot above her lips.

She dressed in black, always: her skirts,
her shirts, tights around thick calves. Her
skewed smile reflected the dark, a personal past
immersed in heavy texts, lecture preparation.

She spoke as if she sang, a deep alto dirge,
the beat of her words, rolled consonants,
a rhythmic chant that lulled the class back
in time to eras when the ancients—Egypt,
Greece, Rome—prevailed.

> *I run, out of breath, past the pond where*
> *a classmate hanged herself from a colonial tree*
> *with the burden of a first year away from home,*
> *perhaps a rumored pregnancy, perhaps a chapel*
> *hymn too heavy to sing. I run, pant, my Bermuda*
> *shorts an itchy reminder of how much I want*
> *to fit in, to be one of the boarding-school girls*
> *who pleases my housemother. Oh how I run,*
> *I'm late—again, again, I never reach the ivied*
> *building in time to take the exam.*

That dream again. I left this place so
long ago, took my Bermudas and my C
in Ancient History, its maroon tome filled
with underlines, dog-ears, my repeated night
terror a reminder of how I could not cope.

Caribbean on the Hudson

What a crew, residents of Caribbean House,
River Road, Edgewater. The five-story building
shone along the Hudson. To the north, the George
Washington Bridge framed Palisades cliffs.

The Caribbean House: five stories, each named
for an island. I lived on Three—Jamaica. My first
apartment as a single teacher, soon to enter the
public relations field, commute to the big city.

My neighbors? Billie on Curaçao, whose talent
was art; she mass-produced inks of stick figures
at cocktail parties, sold them in Village galleries.
Her husband worked long hours so when Gus
on Trinidad developed a fever, Billie took care
of him—very good care.

Down the hall from Gus lived the striking Swede
Bengt, wide shoulders, affable round face, shaved
pate. We called him Mr. Clean because of his uncanny
resemblance to the fellow on the household bottle.

On Bahamas (Barbados?) the twin Mike, whose brother
Don and sister-in-law took over his apartment while their
Manhattan manse underwent renovation. No one could
tell the difference so said *hello Mike* in the elevator to
whichever twin stepped in.

Josie on Aruba, who longed for the days she'd worked
at a New York ad agency, mothered and cooked with
great resentment. One day the black cat dropped from
her fifth-floor balcony and survived, another astronaut
in the age of John Glenn's earth orbit.

A sweet boy named Craig, only eight when his parents
moved to a single-family home so he could run free
with friends, played with a rope and a tree branch.
The Caribbean population, including Larry, the former
priest married to a former nun, all mourned at his wake.

My dear friend Ronne, whose window I overlooked
from mine. I miss her every day.

Miss Glick

When I was a teen, my mother took me
to Manhattan to buy clothes for the new
school year. She took me to Saks, not
the elegant emporium on Fifth, but its
retail seed on Thirty-fourth Street.

Saks 34th—it was Saks, all right but
without the glitz of its retail progeny,
without icicles that hung from first-floor
ceilings every December, without elevator
operators who looked as if they were related
to the Vanderbilts, without Italian wools,
argyle socks, blouses of the sheerest Pima.

Without chic. I didn't know that when
my mother took me to Saks 34th and
gladly wore the cardboard skirt—*this
year's color*, said the saleslady, *charcoal
blue*—and a pink sweater. *Orlon*, she said,
no warning about pills that soon would
erupt on the front—like teenage acne—
over my high-school breasts.

As I grew into the scholar I would become,
Mom worried that I wouldn't marry in time,
though I didn't know in time for what. Just
as I transferred from a school I abhorred
to one I embraced, she and I transferred
to Saks on Fifth, to the seventh floor, where
Miss Glick, dressed in black with sensible
shoes, a doyenne with a Brooklyn tinge
to her Rs, took charge.

You need the right dresses for those young men
who'll soon be chasing you, in three years you'll
be back for your trousseau, she said. Oh how my
mother loved that, only three years to wait, engaged,
married, babies soon after, maybe a house nearby.

Back to Saks in three years, then six, then nine, always
on the prowl for the right dress, like the tight-bodice,
full-skirt design, red wool soft enough to diaper one of
those elusive babies, the dress I wore when I dined
at Brasserie with the radiologist from Washington.
He'd come into town after a hiatus in our romance,
squired me to four plays in as many nights. When we
met someone he knew (a friend of a friend of a friend)
as he ate steak tartare, he told her *no, we're not engaged,*
she's one of the fish I'm dating while I swim in the pond
of fun. A fish! The pond of fun!

And so it went, visits to Miss Glick for dresses: grey,
sleeveless wool with an Empire waist, turquoise Chanel
(a copy) to mimic Jackie. I wore them to theatre, dinners
with dates related to urban mayors, to my married sister's
neighbors, dates I didn't want as one of my own relatives.

A decade after Miss Glick had prophesized my imminent
engagement (a diamond to wear with my cap and gown),
Mom and I went to Manhattan to see our Saks lady, white
curls in threads among her sable tresses. *Finally,* Mom told
this patient woman who'd waited with her for so many years,
finally, the wedding's in ten weeks, look at that ring.

Miss Glick: *See? I told you it would happen, let's get you*
that trousseau. And she went into the back room to see
what she could find.

A Proper Gentleman

After *A Proper Gentleman*
—from *Subway Series,* Marla Del Collins

All that summer I thought the Beatles sang for me: *all you need is love, love, love is all you need.* I'd found my love, a man with a midwest twang who knew every corner of New York, who took me to city spots I'd never seen, though all my life I'd lived along the eastern seaboard. Manhattan, one Saturday night, maybe we watched *The Endless Summer* in the Kips Bay Theatre with the marquee that cautioned *The Endless Summer ends tomorrow.* Then the Second Avenue bus to the Lower East Side, Katz's Delicatessen, where salamis above the counter mimed chandeliers, where tea came in glass tumblers, where corned beef sandwiches promised tomorrow's lunch. We sat at a narrow table, surrounded by a smattering of other Katz late-nighters. The waiter approached, maybe to see if we wanted anything else, but no, instead he said, his voice heavy with his own eastern-Europe salt,

A proper gentleman
Would not block the aisle
With his long leg. Move it

Dressed for Life

Sometimes she takes beautiful me from the closet to try me on. *It still fits*, she tells her reflection. *Very Madmen*, says her daughter. I've traveled with her to three homes, to dwell in darkness of three closets with other memories. She couldn't afford me then, she couldn't now, but you should have seen her mother's face when she pulled me over her head, zipped me, said *I love it, I love it*, and even though my name was French—Louis Fereaud—and I cost almost as much as her wedding gown from Henri Bendel on Fifty-seventh, I found myself in a garment bag. Her going-away dress. I'd take her to her new life with the man in the white dinner jacket after a night of chateaubriand and baked Alaska, after the last photo where he'd lifted her high in his arms under the synagogue awning, her veil like wings behind her. I'd waited on her bed where she'd slept alone the night before and then: she rushed in, traded the gown for elegant me, black and white silk with red flower buttons. She laid the veil on the pillow, tossed her sling-backs to the floor, slipped into white patent leather pumps, picked up the matching purse, knelt down to kiss her Boston terrier goodbye, and rode off to the Saddle Brook Marriott, ten minutes away, where I deferred to the pink gauze peignoir she preferred.

What Did They Learn from Me?

I wonder if any of them became poets,
the students I taught in my first married year.

Linda, quick to tell all that her father
built a private room in the attic, where
her mother served his dinner, where he
read under a single bulb, where he slept
most nights.

Stephen, who mimed reproach, his mouth
molding the words seconds after I'd chastised
him, who told me in a plaintive lisp that he
could not stay for detention, his mother
wouldn't let him cross Sycamore Street alone.

Philip, one of nine siblings, the example I cited
when the principal told me I could not teach
throughout my pregnancy. *School policy*, he said,
these children shouldn't see you in that condition.

Richard, with cobalt eyes and enviable lashes
that defied nature, who revealed as tears wet
those eyes that the baby I carried under my
miniskirt tent dress was doomed, the other
children told him I carried a dragon within.
When his Army father transferred the family
to Japan, he sent me a bib, a golden dragon
stitched across silken ruffles.

Randy, whose fury prompted him to punch
a visitor in the gut, whose parents could not
accept his demons.

Do they write about the father in the attic,
the terror of crossing a quiet suburban street,
the teacher who carried a dragon almost
to term in front of their eight-year-old eyes?
Perhaps they write about the Friday spelling tests,
new words not memorized from lists, the tests
that brought Jonathan's mother to the school
on Sycamore Street to lodge a complaint.

Generations

After *Origins III—High Contrast Karma,* Gia Coppola

Hot night, our apartment unbearable, flash storms
flood the creek below, no relief. On the television
screen a blurred shadow—like a robot, he bounces
on his trampoline: the moon. The moon! My belly,
earthbound orb, protects our daughter, her birth
two months away. *We can do anything,* I think,
walk on the moon, bring life into the world. How
peaceful Neil Armstrong looks, how frightened
his wife must have been. (I'm frightened too.)
September at the Smithsonian, we view a moon
rock behind glass, protected like the girl named
Karen who would make her first voyage, a giant
leap into our lives five days later.

After *Tea Time,* Vladimir Volegov

We never had time for tea parties, my daughters
and I, too busy with spaghetti, *I like Aunt Millie's
Sauce,* Kate would say. Many days, before school
let out, piano carpools, rehearsals, I drove the half
hour to Paterson, picked up my mother, took a trip
to the cemetery to visit my dad, to the Grand Union,
to her doctor, then to IHOP to share silver dollars
or Swedish pancake rollups. I'd drop her outside
her high rise, its New York skyline view now
hidden by a sister building.
 Come in, it's winter
 Have a hot cup of tea,
 Ma, it's late.
We never had time for tea parties either.

Afloat

Mommy, come quick, Nana's taking a bath
with twenty-dollar bills. Lots of them.

We're in Puerto Rico, guests of my mom at a
furniture-movers convention, a club of men that
included my dad until his early death a half dozen
years earlier. The group still adored her. *Cele, you*
need to be with us, the caller would say, *Cele, we*
have a watch engraved with your name, you ran
the business with Ben, come, bring your children.

At this island retreat, miles away from the clamor
of San Juan, my girls share her room, sometimes
breakfast with her while their father and I pretend
we're on our honeymoon, the tryst we missed
in the tumult of the sixties, the draft at our door.

Hurry, Mommy, come see the money. I hear my
mother's raucous guffaws from the tub, the tepid
liquid an antidote to her day in the sun. It's dusk,
the cocktail hour awaits, I need to dress, she needs
to dress, to show off her granddaughters.

Still wearing glasses, she sits in the tub, unashamed
of her breasts like large U's perched atop the water,
the rest of her womanhood hidden with bubbles from
the miniature hotel bottle. Wads of twenties, tens,
a few ones, swim around her, the day's currency
cache that stuck to her sweaty waist as she took
off her corset (no bathing suit for this non-swimmer).

In the adjoining room, my husband listens to levity
as four giddy girls embrace their connection, wired
together by genetics, a connection that would end
too soon, that let us laugh while we could.

Slick: a Love Story

Chicken soup, the holiday's here, right?
That's what Slick the plumber would say
twice a year as he lay prone on my kitchen
floor, cleaning out the clog in the disposal—
peels of parsnips, onions, leeks, carrots,
turnips, fibrous stems of fresh dill.

Slick, name that stuck to him like Elmer's Glue
well into his octogenarian years, when getting
down to view the cavern of vegetable carnage
became a challenge. Arthritic knees belied the lank
teen who'd evaded the police as he slithered away
like a greased pig when mischief marked his
reputation, his full head of jet hair the only
flash as he fled through the streets of town.

This oversized scamp-turned-man never married
and as he aged, he cared for his ailing sister in a
home near the church where he attended daily Mass.
He'd appear minutes after a frantic call—*Slick,
the disposal, hurry, guests on the way*—lower
his old balding self, flashlight in hand, to install
wider pipes under the sink, sometimes to mount
a ladder in search of the source along the garage
wall, where pipes rebelled at the touch of his wrench,
spewed slop on this wet warrior—unfazed, dedicated.

Gentle Slick who visited whenever puppies were born
to watch them suckle, quiver in their sleep, tears in his
eyes at life's miracle. Chivalrous Slick who took a shovel,
lifted the dead bunny from the driveway, reverently placed
it in a bag-turned-coffin, its last rites tendered by his soft

hand. Quasi mayor Slick who held court nightly in our town's diner, sat with his back to the counter near the door, greeted familiar faces, made new friends, his gap-toothed smile a radiance.

When Slick died, the church that may have hidden the teen hooligan, the church where he prayed every morning before helping housewives of New Jersey clear their paths, that church was filled to the apse with a host of dedicated admirers who miss him still.

The Tablecloth

Decades of dinners sat on the tablecloth, cream
brocade with indelible spots: soup spills, briskets,
turkey gravy, an everlasting stew served up with
debate, whining, laughter, dog yelps from the kitchen,
let me out, I don't belong in this crate.

One March Passover, winter's last shot, a half foot
of snow the day before, so many still with us—my
mother, my husband's parents, our friends, their
parents. We watched them slide down the driveway,
casseroles in hand. Through the cluttered garage they
snaked around parked cars, bikes, striped beach chairs
that longed for summer.

Their coats shed, we gathered around the table,
fifteen crowded where twelve could fit. My husband
dimmed the lights, began a slide show. For months
he'd copied family photos of all present, set slides to
music. He featured the elders as young lovers, showed
hopeful brides, grooms, showed the children (to their
delight) as newborns, toddlers, pre-teens.

The kids cackled at their parents as kids; grandparents
wept for sweet memories (my mother for her husband),
the middle generation watchful for the present, fearful
of the future.

The tablecloth heard a lot that night. *The matzoh balls
are too hard. Too soft. You'll be eating this brisket
for a week. So freeze it. I can't eat another thing.*
And then it heard goodbyes. Time for our friends
to return parents to their nest three towns away.

The tablecloth saw many festive occasions after that, witnessed gatherings when our daughters' grandparents died. Sometimes other cloths, sewn on the machine upstairs, supplanted its perch. One memorable fabric, aglow with protective coating, repelled liquid. Spills beaded and ran down ten feet of table, the direction depending on which way laughing cousins tilted it.

But this veteran was the favorite, spots masked by centerpieces, service plates, mismatched water goblets. Shreds lovingly patched, its life paralleled by personal growth, its burdens lightened by hungry boyfriends.

Replaced by more splendid cloths, one brought by our daughter from her honeymoon, it was relegated to the back of the linen shelf. Until the garage sale. Pulled out, washed, tumbled, pressed, tied with a gold bow, it lay regally in the driveway on the ping-pong table, stood inspection by seasoned garagers.

The familiar family laughter distant, it listened anew. *Why only seven napkins? What's this spot? Wouldja take two dollars? How about throwing in these placemats?*

And I answered: *It's been sold.*

Budapest, 1983

Hope

The Soviet monument looms in a park (I don't remember if it was Buda or Pest), smiling nuns and school children pose in front, the next group awaits. A museum nearby spotlights war, industry, *progress*. We visit the home where Dr. Semmelweis lived, his findings on childbirth fever rejected by the medical community— until they weren't. At the Forum Hotel on the Danube, indoor pool water, bath-warm, almost black, invites us for a midday swim before the dining room buffet, chicken paprikash, the real thing, red, tangy on the tongue. At night under a feather comforter, we watch *Die Fleidermaus,* a repeat from the Vienna Opera, on the tiny television's only channel. Static snow cascades over the frolicking cast, audience laughter resounds. Near midnight the bars along the riverbank come alive with the looming lava of change, dance music and youthful voices that herald the statue's toppled demise six years later. We board the bus in morning, head back to Vienna through fields of sunflowers that swirl like a lemon silk dress on the landscape.

Shadows

As we stand on Dohány Street, gaze in awe at the
Great Synagogue, a bent man slips from the shadows,
his belongings in a wagon, his arms (he shows us)
a fire-scarred map with numbers that tell where he's been.

He speaks Yiddish; we understand some, his gestures close
the gap. He leads us on an unexpected tour: *here*, he tells us,
*is the street where the rabbi lived, where they pulled him out,
took him with all the others. Here,* he points, *is the cemetery.*
We see headstones, a congregation of blessed memory.
His wife—*vayb*—sent to the camps, the women's side,
no stone to mark her ashen grave.

There, he waves toward the synagogue, *there we prayed*
before they came, before they forced us from our homes.
He stretches his arms forward, like the number eleven,
like a blessing, then clenches his fists, captures the scene
that burns his brain.

Gone, gone, the Jews—taken.
The Jews—gone.

We listen to his truths. Then his name, I print it in
our Berlitz guide—*Binyamin Cohen.* Benjamin, my
beloved father's name, my grandson's name now.
We press American dollars into his waiting hand
before he glides back into the shadows.

For Jordan: Seasons, 2013

Our praise to You . . . for giving us life, sustaining us,
and enabling us to reach this season
—from Shehecheyanu prayer, Talmud

Morning: Let Us Pray

Your young friends in the back rows are silent,
maybe on muted cellphones, perhaps as rapt
as I am while I watch you, listen to you chant.

The dusk you came to us, a Caesarean delivery
after so many hours, you looked at me through
the goo they'd slathered on your eyes, you didn't
cry, not then, you simply stared at this tall woman
whose arms you trusted without choice, whose own
eyes would watch you bloom for these thirteen years,
could you feel my love?

On this equinox weekend, you sing from the Torah
without fault, you tell all how you intend to carry it
in your heart, in your deeds. From my front row seat,
better than any Broadway orchestra ticket, I hear you
thank those who brought you to this day.

Little boy grown taller than most boys your age, in your
newfound voice, so deep, you gently chide me, repeat
advice you've heard from me, you call me *my short,*
short Nana, the congregation chuckles, we lock love
eyes, and I wish I could cradle you again as I did that
first night when I felt so very tall.

Night: My Grandson Knows How to Slow Dance

As we enter the venue, we hear music so loud we are
forced to use hand gestures, facial expressions, for the
rest of the night. On a platform, a gaggle of gawky teens
bends forward, backward, they rock in synchrony as if
on toy ponies, boys in bold stripes, pink shirts, khakis.
Girls in black minis, tiny shoulder straps, totter on silver
heels they'd never worn before.

They rock through the night, they gather around while
the boy of the hour calls up family and friends to light
candles on blue bar mitzvah cupcakes. So many children,
we can't see him in the group, we're reminded of the Waldo
books where we'd searched for the character in red and white.

I wonder where indeed is Waldo, the toddler who clasped
my hand on the street, said *hurry hurry* on Lunch with
the Librarian Tuesdays, picture books and peanut butter
in the summer arbor. Where's Waldo who celebrated
each birthday with a photo, my chin perched on his head,
my arms around his narrow shoulders? Where's this Waldo
who captures swim titles, shoulders now widened to power
his arms through chlorinated lanes?

Oh, there he is, lights suddenly soft, music suddenly
slowed. I watch him, so happy as he holds his girl by
her waist, as she smiles at him through braces as they
dance—as if there is no one else in the room.

For Ben: A Year to Remember, 2014

Halls

I see you enter from the synagogue hallway,
a slight swagger to your gait, your comfort level
a ten on the scale. The cantor invites you to remove
the scroll from the ark, to unroll it, expose this day's
portion. Photographs: we quickly form family groups,
snap snap, our own cameras capture these scenes.

The sanctuary fills, your friends up front, five times
ten and more. And so it begins, your day to glow,
to captivate us. You chant the story of Moses, his
last days, you glide through, deft as an ice skater,
the music of our faith rises, falls, we wonder how
time took us here so fast.

The record-hot day you came home from the hospital
in lime-green overalls, your mom carried you down the
hall to your apartment, the red ribbon of life already tied
around the doorknob. Neighbors in the courtyard, their
toddlers in a plastic pool you'd someday test, waved,
marveled at your size, perhaps remembered their own
walks down that hall, the welcome burden of raising
a child paramount in their thoughts.

So many halls to walk down, dear grandson, may today's
be one blessing among the braided paths that beckon.

Cousins

He'll be home next Sunday, says my daughter,
who watched her son board a plane destined
for Israel. When she told us he would go,
my what-ifs kicked in, properly accompanied
by palpitations, shortness of breath.

What if the plane's de-icer doesn't work?
What if there's a terrorist aboard?
What if he steps too close to Masada's edge?

What if, what if, what if?

Two nights, says the synagogue letter, *there are*
two nights when students can meet with relatives.
I think of my cousin Hadassa, We meet on Skype,
share distant lives. Despite what-ifs, she and her
mother roamed during the war, slept in barns,
railway stations, evaded extermination, while her
grandparents, baby sister, the six million, perished.
Four years, then freedom—Israel.

Hadassa, Ben, Ben, Hadassa.

Elaborate plans, her cell number, the rabbi's
cell number, photos exchanged, a test drive
to find the hotel days before. They arrive,
Hadassa, her husband Yacov. Here at home
In New Jersey, wind-lapped snow outside,
I wait with my laptop. Skype chimes hello.
There they are—my grandson, my cousin, her
husband. Ben tells me he ate Margarita pizza,
he's happy, he's tired, he's in a restaurant booth
next to her, he's my surrogate for the trip I may
never take.

Give her a hug for me, I tell him.

For Brandon: Parking 101

Last space, two white lines.
    Easy.
Two white lines, park here,
pull between two white lines,
easy, basketball boy in the back
seat. Raindrops the size of Liz
Taylor gems pelt the roof.

I'm in.
    Get out of the car,
    get out of the car.
Look. I'm on the left line.
    Get into the car,
    get into the car.
    Belt in, hurry hurry, late late.

Back up, slow down, watch the van
on the right, car behind wants the space.
    No way.
Belt in belt in, pull up between two lines.
Easy. Unbelt, get out of the car,
rain, umbrella, slam doors.

Look—on the right line now.
    How?
Get into the car, belt in,
hurry hurry, late late.

Third try, pull in—done.

I ask him, *when you are old enough to drive,
do you want me to teach you how to park?*

His eyes roll back behind his forehead.

I'd rather be taught by a duck, he says.

For Liv: Blazon as She Turns Eleven

You are my *smoothie*
—you churn, you blend,
   you fill my glass with joy

You are my *sunrise*
—your brightness lights
   my sky each time you're near

You are my *cartwheel*
—you lead my life to
   unexpected twirls

You are my *backbend*
—you turn an upside-down
   world right side up

You are my *magazine*
—your pages flip, inform
   me as you grow

You are my *goldfinch*
—you gleam, you fly,
   you bring me wonder

You are my *smoothie*
—you churn, you blend,
   you fill my glass with joy

To My Lost Town

Don't take the boys there, says my daughter, *street crime, drug dealers, shootings*. The boys, fresh from the summer's first swim meet, take the cue. *We don't want to go, we're tired, we're scared*, they say, then return to their handhelds, play games. We stand firm, feed them, leave for Paterson. They protest yet know we won't back down. Once there we park near the Great Falls. *Wait for us*, we caution, *don't walk by yourselves*. The parking lot is near empty on this hot June day, but once they see the water cascade over the cliffs—water that powered an industry, water that immigrant boys their ages heard from nearby mills, water with a song that accompanied the churn of machines—they run to the edge of the little plaza, now a national historic park, leap atop slatted benches, jump down to peer through chain-link holes, their phones now morphed into cameras to record the core of a city that shimmered for generations they'll never meet.

Two Dogs

Schepseleh

The winter before he turned fifteen, our dog sat on my lap,
offered kisses, his Mr. Hyde personality obscured by sudden
passion. Surprised by his ardor, I curled my hands around
his neck, massaged his coarse hair, baby-talked his name,
asked him if, after all this time, he really loved me. That's
when I felt the hard lump. *It's nothing*, I told myself, older
dogs get lumps, he'd just run up the deck stairs in the snow.
But no, the vet told me the next day, as she pointed out the
lump near his rear leg, lumps in other crooks I feared to
touch, lumps that proved his impending departure. He lived
three months longer, long enough to chase squirrels from
the bird feeder outside the kitchen door, not long enough
to welcome fifteen with a candle atop his hamburger.

Eliza Jane

She doesn't know she's ill, her short
breaths at the top of the stairs now an
everyday sign.

She doesn't know our fear, that one
morning we'll come downstairs, find
her lifeless or worse—know that we've
come to the day of decision.

She waits for her meds, wrapped in
Velveeta, we're thankful she's made
it to another slice, that she still tries to
leap onto the sofa, that she dines with
gusto. She doesn't know, doesn't
know, but we do.

Old Bags

Hadassa's painting *My Old Handbags*—delicate jeweled
purses—reminds me of my mother's beaded collection.
In a bottom dresser drawer, these treasures lie dormant,

gems that took her with my father to now-decayed
Catskills resorts, that flew with her as a business wife
to convention galas on humid islands, that adorned

her sequined gowns at winter dances in ballrooms
long before the days of Judith Lieber. I owned a few
flashy evening bags as well, one gold mesh, so tiny

even a faerie's comb couldn't fit, but ample enough
for the mad money Mama provided—*in case your date
gets fresh and you need to call Daddy.* I never used the

mad money, yet sometimes when I peer inside at the old
bags in my bottom drawer among the tangled costume
bracelets my second-graders thought I might like to wear,

I spot a nickel, remember a phone booth on the corner
next to a domed synagogue. There I am! In a cantaloupe
cashmere shirtdress from Mikola's on Broadway, black

patent-leather high-heeled pumps over Hanes hose.
I see the ghosts of Paterson, warm and smiling as they
fox-trot around a parquet floor now dulled, abandoned

along with the stage where a band once played.

What I Don't Know

I didn't think to ask
    where your steamship ported, was it Baltimore?
      Galveston? Philadelphia?
    why your family moved from town to town after
      you debarked
    how you met my father

I didn't think to ask
    how it felt to lose three sons before you could
      give them life
    how it felt to lose your mother as she
      played cards with my sister
    how it felt to birth me a year after she died

I didn't think to ask
    if you were pregnant in the photo marked
      Lovingly Yours
    if you ever learned to drive
    why you gave up the wheel if you did

I didn't ask
    how you knew your sister, your brother,
      were dead in the camps
    how you felt when you heard that news
    how you could breathe and go on

Mama, I ask you now, should I offer my daughters
answers to questions they haven't thought to ask?

Quiet

She never told me
to go to Palisades Park,
too dangerous, she said.

She never told me
to say no to a blind date,
how will you find a husband, she said.

He never told me
to go ahead, be a veterinarian,
girls should be teachers, nurses, he said.

He never told me
why she left for days at a time,
she'll be back soon, he said.

She never told me
how she heard about her brother, her sister,
they died in the camps, she said.

She never told me
why she lost those babies,
they all were boys, she said.

He never told me
why he became so sad,
do you like my new car, he said.

I never told them
how much I loved them.

The Walk

August night, outdoor diners wind down,
tacos under tarps, pasta next to car exhaust,
Mojitos, mosquitos. Bars, four to a square
block, spill drinkers to the street, smokers

cloud sidewalks, music blasts past bouncers
at open doors, neighbors from upscale condos
at council meetings: *the noise, please, we didn't*

count on the noise. We walk through town, two
survivors who talk about anything but illness,
dog on lead, plastic ShopRite bag in pocket

just in case. Strollers in tandem bend to pet her,
oh look how she wags her tail, is she friendly?
Four pompous pups, chests puffed out, lunge on
leashes, their owners command: *sit, stay, down.*

We dance around them, *good dog, good dog,*
good dog, good dog, the two men sing, nod their
heads toward sienna slickness held tight on spiked

collars. We avoid side streets with empty offices, skirt
the park with the lush fountain, we can hear arguments
inside, secrets spew between oaks. We pass the studio

where we could learn how to pole dance (two survivors
laugh at the idea), we pass the building where films light
up the side on other nights like these, the town's children
in awe of Disney characters on brick walls. In the dark

on the lawn of the church where high gargoyles cool their
stone noses, a Husky's white face glows neon. His owner
bends to find what lies in the grass, his wife, next to us

on the sidewalk, chants *give me the bag. Why*, he wants
to know. *Just. Give. Me. The bag,* she says. August night,
a walk through town, two survivors, thankful, reach the car.

The Pose

After *Unconditional Surrender*
—Seward Johnson, Styrofoam, 2005

Eeww, says my pubescent grandson, *that's so
embarrassing, how can you do that?* He's just
seen our photo as we emulate the sailor and nurse,
V-J Day strangers who embraced in Times Square
to celebrate victory, dominance, the promise
of peace in a world history that knew none,
knows none, foresees none.

We pose through our hope, our love, only days
before an anniversary that races toward a half
century, a marriage that celebrates our victory,
our dominance in the face of lost loved ones,
our endurance that now holds the promise of
less time when we'd felt there was infinity.

Invited by magnitude, spurred by abandon
that a day amid joy can produce, we pose
like the couple whose image we'd snapped
minutes earlier. I hand them my iPhone,
no thought of the conflict the Times Square
photo caused among those who claimed fame:
I was that nurse, I was that sailor.

Yet there at Grounds for Sculpture and the roads
that surround, there is peace. Static scenes: lakeside
picnickers, bronze teenage boys who lust after
a stilled reader, her girlhood in bloom, mammoth
Marilyn who peers over the tree line, beckons,
come closer, touch my red toes, lean on my legs.

Daredevil children atop a tall building across
the road surely frolic through thunderstorms,
bullfrogs croon love songs among water lilies,
and we wonder if the artworks speak to each other
in night's blackness about humans in summer shorts
who—fueled by blazing sun—wander among them,
pose without shame because the art has set them free.

Why I Can't Part with Fisher-Price People

There they sit, six tiny wooden students in a bus bound for the little
schoolhouse with a bell on the roof. Actually two schoolhouses,
one found at a garage sale, only a dollar. Little wooden people,
smiles painted on face orbs, they've just come from the dollhouse,
four rooms for a whole family, a staircase that leads to Anywhere.
The airport and its plane perch close by, the sexless pilot in a cap
that matches his cloudless yonder snug in the cockpit hole, his
happy passengers behind, ready for takeoff. The hospital staff
awaits trauma, Lucky the dog pops up, down, in the lawnmower,
the wagon that carried blocks lies in the toy chest next to the Jolly
Jalopy, clown as driver. I found these in our basement among
detritus of decades, treasures that my daughters relished, that my
husband placed on our bedroom floor when he declared Saturday
Fisher-Price Day, spread the assortment out for two little girls
whose imaginations worked overtime in a world populated by tiny
people. I found them, set them out in a corner of the den, listened
to grandchildren fancy other worlds on their own Fisher-Price
days. The make-believe village remained in the corner as these
young ones outgrew their imaginations, abandoned peeling
buildings. It's time to let them go, symbols that inspired a theatre
where tickets were free, where ageless actors were wooden, their
dialogues always new.

Pelicans at Sunrise

Just before sunrise at Sanibel,
pelicans gather, soar high above
the Gulf, then dive and soar again.

My high school friend swam in waters
like these as a young man. Awed by an
avian fisherman that could gulp whole
fish into a waiting gullet, he squinted
toward the sun, unaware that this circling
hunter would swoop down, pluck out
his eye.

He married much later than the rest of us,
chatted at class reunions about his progeny
as the youngest: ours were wed and parents,
his just starting their college days.

We never could tell which eye was taken,
they seemed alike, it would have been rude
to stare, but the incident was the icon
that defined him throughout his life.

You remember, we'd say when he was
out of range, *a pelican took out his eye*.
When I read about his passing a few years
ago, I recalled a sweet man, bespectacled,
who didn't seem his age, whose generous
smiles belied his trials, who gave his eye to
a pelican and never looked back.

Where are the Hens?

In our hotel room four floors above Duval Street,
we leave our dreams behind as the six a.m. rooster
crows. The roosters of Key West roam free along

the streets, peck at gutter crumbs, call to each other
from alleys where bicycles—many pink—lean against
picket fences that surround balconied homes. Waves

of tourists ooze along America's southernmost lanes,
side-step the kings whose scarlet crowns wiggle in the
wind while they call for brethren to join the parade.

We of course think of that old joke—*Why did the
chicken cross the road?*—and wonder why a town
where many entrées cost in the range of thirty dollars

supports this population, descended, they say, from
Cubalaya, fighting cocks brought from the island
ninety miles away long before missile threats.

No more clawed combat except among residents who
either want the roosters to remain or to leave. (How?)
I read there are safe houses for these birds, and as we

watch traffic stop—*I brake for roosters*—we can see
which faction is ahead. We dine al fresco next to
crowing fowl, we heed their calls outside the home

where Hemingway penned his thoughts, we walk up
Duval, cross Fleming, trek from waterside to waterside
in minutes, we marvel at blue butterflies that flit for their

two weeks of life in a safe conservatory, and we pull out
pocket digitals to record a dot on the map where opulence
meets untamed as the roosters rule the streets of Key West.

Cats of Whitehead Street

In the living room, Benny Goodman suns himself, the window screen forms lattice patterns over his nose. His brother Fats Waller wallows on the sofa (*Don't sit here*, says the sign) while Humphrey Bogart begs for breakfast treats. Elizabeth Taylor, eyes not violet but green, leaps to her pedestal to get a better view of adoring crowds who hear that she birthed Etta James, Tennessee Williams, and Mata Hari. Like her feline housemates, Elizabeth sports six digits on her paws. Her social circle holds at forty-five for now, some redheads, others tinted shades of grey, others coal black like the original Liz's tresses. We follow into a bedroom where Captain Tony lolls on the white bedspread, an antique chair (for birth, they say) nearby. A team of tourists snakes through the garden, circles the pool (almost thirty-thousand dollars in '38). Along a path near the cemetery where Frank Sinatra and Zsa Zsa Gabor join Willard Scott for eternity, a wandering Calico, perhaps pregnant but not in need of a birthing chair, silently sidles a nearby leg. The shade of an African tulip tree tempers noontime heat as we record the joy of visiting Hemingway's Key West home, where heirs of Snowball, his good-luck gift from a ship's captain, own the grounds.

Roll 'em

Hollywood soothes me with Tom Hanks
and Meg Ryan, the cutest pair ever to
not know that even though they hate
each other, they've found love in simpatico
online chats. Bing! You've got mail!

Where has that film gone? A year since
I last found it, oh how I miss Meg's *I wanted
it to be you so badly* before Tom tells her
Don't cry (pause) *Shopgirl,* wipes her eyes
with his folded handkerchief, kisses her with
pent-up passion while "Over the Rainbow"
blares around them in a flower-filled Manhattan
park, no one else in sight. An affable retriever,
teeth on Tom's jacket, barks the rhythm. Cut to
cloudless sky . . . *The End.*

Newness unnerves me. I seek solace from the familiar:
reruns, frayed blankets, warmth from the sofa corner
shaped by the weight of my curled body in torn pajama
bottoms and a ragged t-shirt that boasts *I rode the steam
train through the Sierras.*

Meg and Tom, come back to the den. Comfort me.

It's All There

The friends we have made we will always remember
—Camp Lincoln-Laurel alma mater

I find the perfect birthday card for you, my pal of so many
decades. It shows two old women: the smiler who professes
her forever friendship, the frowner who asks, *Who are you
and why is your hand on my shoulder?*

Inside the card, on the blank side, I create a birthday
game, jot stanzas of our camp alma mater, insert blanks
where words used to be, words I've forgotten, like when
I couldn't recall *cilantro* or *tank top*. I'd panicked, the gap
in my brain as vacant as steppes of Russia.

I call you and as usual, start in the midst of an ongoing
conversation we continue to embellish with rowdy laughter.
We sing, piece together fragments, decide to email the camp
owners' daughters. Online in the white pages, I locate George,
the music counselor who cast me in Broadway shows (albeit it
in the far reaches of New Jersey).

Missives fly back and forth, the computer links us all,
compresses time, we're young again, we gather missing
phrases, fill in patches with *thoughts we will keep through
the cold of December . . . Em'rald pines and skies of blue.*
George scans, emails the notes, says *be sure to sing the B-flat.*

We piece together a musical tribute to a place where we felt
safe, we sing of *pleasures sweeter than the top of a cake,*
of friendships deep as the lake long abandoned by the aging
population that can't always remember, that tries not to forget.

Mrs. Piggle-Wiggle

These mornings I put three cinnamon sticks
in the Wearever percolator atop the stove,
cinnamon for the flavor, cinnamon for my
heart's hairline vessels.

Mrs. Piggle–Wiggle didn't care about her arteries,
she cared about the town's children who'd flock
to her upside-down house on the way home from school.
No track team, no soccer, no debates to distract them
from this humpbacked lady who wore a tiara, whose
home smelled from cinnamon-sugar cookies fresh
from the oven.

The children dressed in costumes, dug for buried
treasure in her back yard, downed snacks, unaware
of allergies, unable to text their mothers, *I'm at Mrs.
Piggle-Wiggle's*, they'd type if they could.

The mothers in town called Mrs. Piggle-Wiggle,
childless herself, for advice—a daughter who
wouldn't eat, a son whose toys blocked the
entrance to his room, the twins who bickered
endlessly. And this chubby lady without a graduate
degree in psychology offered sure solutions, like
Penelope the parrot who moved in with Mary's
family, repeated this answer-backer's snide sasses
until Mary was *cured*.

For my eighth birthday, my friend Marcia gave me
a blue book reread so often that yellowed pages hold
stains. (*Don't read at the table*, my mother said.) When
I read the stories I treasured to my grandchildren, they
wondered at the idea of a nosy lady whose place
wouldn't be considered a safe haven today.

Believe Me

I'll tell friends I haven't phoned because I found a fare bargain
for El Al, flew to Israel to visit my cousin. I didn't have time
to call her or write, my visit will be a surprise. On Skype,
for four years she tells me *come, we have room, come before
we are both too old, before it's too late.*

I'm on the plane, bumped to first class, St. Peter's Fish from
the Sea of Galilee, eggplant, black tomatoes, Champagne from
the vineyards atop Mount Carmel. Israeli dance music pipes
into my headset, lulls me to sleep. I dream, how nice it would
be to take my mother.

I'll tell everyone that my mother joined me, we fly together,
two angels, though she remains terrified of flight as she was
in life. We land in Tel Aviv, step into a cab headed for Netanya,
to the beach across from my cousin's high-rise. She's on the
balcony, her binoculars trained toward the sea.

She spies us. *Aunt Cele*, she calls to my mother, and in minutes
she skates across the roadway, flowers in hand, her cheeks smooth
as in her long-ago bridal portrait. *Aunt Cele, how did you come
back, did you see my grandmother, your sister in Eternity, sent
to the Ghetto, murdered?*   To me: *I told you we have room.*

Vapor

After *The Three Fates (Working Title)*
—Seward Johnson, Aluminum and Foam, 2011

Three Fates or Hags or Witches, call them all;
They boil a cauldron filled with feet and brains,
A fenny snake, its venom's pow'r forestalled,
And hollowed eyes and toes from lives well drained.
Who are these Fates, and why are they portrayed?
What do they think as throngs walk by their site?
And why were kings and nobles so dismayed
While little children giggled with delight?
And why am I so sad to light on them?
Why fear, why yearn for times I spent in class
When time stretched wide? My studies mattered then;
I'm trapped by years like vapor that has passed.
So boil and bubble, Fates, my pot awaits—
But hark, my ending do not annotate.

They Wait

Ambush

Say you wait by the telephone to hear the news.
Do you really want to answer? Wouldn't it be better
if someone else took the call? What if it's good?
Own it. What if the news is half good, half bad?
Which half will you swallow and how can you spit
out the rest without being called a fool? Say the phone
doesn't ring, you've spent light and dark at the wait.
Say you decide to wash away the call with a glass
of water, a pill, a pillow, a warm blanket, the ringer
turned off, your book on the floor next to the bed.
Say you hear the phone in the distance, you pick up
the extension, someone tells you that you dodged
a bullet. Who aimed the gun?

Night Journey

Yes, time to release rancor, time grows on itself,
pulls me toward the Light, where forgiveness clothes
those who wait. Yes, I try to sleep, the glow a wave,
elusive. Who are these souls? They skim the ceiling,
street fluorescence dances through panes, becomes their
sun. Yes, the bed sheets, cool in summer night. My face
sinks into the gauze abyss, skeletons mock my fear. I
reach for the Light, then turn. It's time—it's not.

The Visit

Late at night in the ICU, she came, sat side-saddle
in a corner chair, as in the photograph taken so long
ago, maybe in the Catskills, her mouth curved in a coy

smile, her round beaded purse at her side, a Chesterfield
askew between nicotine-stained fingers. She didn't beckon
or reach out to ask me to join her, simply perched in the dark
on that chair, the first time I'd seen her in three decades,
my last vision as she lay in her own ICU bed, between lives,
set to leave.

Mama, thank you for coming, I'm not ready.

My Paterson

It wasn't a beautiful street, not from the
eyes of a child afraid to trek the five blocks
to school. On the corner of Twelfth Avenue
waited Marguerite, seventh-grader, bully
before the word became part of the vernacular.
She stood legs apart, hands on hips, lip curled,
the curb's edge a wall behind her.

It wasn't a beautiful house, the two-family shingled
box with trucks in the driveway on a busy through
street, its median filled with weeds, a barrier that
hinted danger across the divide. *You can't cross there,*
my mother warned, *the men who work in the auto
shop are bad, those children in the grey house are
dirty, their mother stays out all night.*

It wasn't a beautiful town, the shops that lined the
main street varied heights, logos emblazoned on brick
sides still visible though the wares inside departed long
ago for more beautiful towns, for malls that caused an
exodus matched by aging towns across the state.

It wasn't a beautiful town but it spawned a generation
that extols its birthplace, that continues to revisit
its streets, that remembers beautiful times.

Our Town, Revived

Now on Facebook, *Jewish Roots in Paterson.*
Paterson: Silk City gone sad, once home to Jews
by the thousands: shopkeepers, attorneys, physicians,
clergy, many from The Old Country, men and women
who kept this town humming. My own father Ben,
a *moving man*, sent his trucks in all directions to carry
furniture, sometimes to another neighborhood, from
flats in two-story homes to ranches, split-levels,
Italianate marble near Eastside Park.

Where dress salons, shoe stores, haberdasheries
stood (five along one of the shorter downtown
streets), there rose bail-bond stores. Where a movie
theatre once enchanted us, we see rubble in the lobby.
In the glorious synagogue where I walked down the
bridal aisle under a stained-glass star, prayers no more.
The gilded art deco choir loft where the hired alto
stunned us with her strength: an empty cavern.
The promenade in front where we claimed our
high school crushes: cracked, dry grass.

But we come alive again on *Jewish Roots*—someone
poses a question, *do you remember this school, that shul,
this house, that deli?* A diligent member drives around town,
photographs homes, our old addresses. Oh, the comments:
*I remember your mother, your dog, we rode the bus to day
camp together, I can't believe we live just two towns apart.*

Whispers from the group that started out with a handful
turn into shouts from a membership that bursts with
familiarity. One thousand voices now call out to each other
to hold on to memories that wrap us in a single warm coat
on days that turn cold.

Resignation

I wanted to play the mandolin, golden
spruce smooth as satin, my fingers easily
stretch along frets. I tilt my head just enough
to allow chestnut tresses to brush my shoulder,
carefully coax quivering sounds,
but—
>   I'll never play the mandolin.

I wanted to craft a Pulitzer novel,
reviewers marveling at my imagery,
my ability to weave fiction into a
tome of historical accuracy. Advances
fill my coffer, allow me to hire a laundress
who keeps me in clean underwear for
my next book signing,
but—
>   I'll never write that novel.

I wanted to stand onstage, footlights
reflecting rouged lips as I bow from
the waist, adored for the show, written,
directed, acted by *me*, an hour and a half
of pained monologues about elusive paths,
but—
>   I'll never stand onstage

Listen.
Can you hear the applause?

Epilogue: Crowns

On the top shelf in my daughter's closet in a room
where she hasn't lived for over a quarter century,
where college texts still line the walls, where Benetton
sweaters we bought in Rome languish in their pilled
state—on that shelf I store two boxes. A pink square
with shredded brown string, and a navy oval, its sheen
faded. Not from the girl who shopped in that closet
daily before she left for high school in the ghostly
face powder and jet eye liner that appalled her father.

The boxes: traces of my mother, hats from Jean's
Millinery, 17 Church Street, Paterson, *Known For
Exclusive Les Chapeaux*, the lid says. More hats
from Maxine's in Passaic, 701 Main Avenue. And
inside? Treasures worth more per ounce than the price
of gold. Hats with demure veils that hid eyes worn by
dawn drudgery, dispatching her husband's moving vans,
by two daughters who needed attention, by hot meals
served at noon on oilcloth in the kitchen. By knowledge
of those taken by the unspeakable, led without protest
to uncharted graves.

The hats: brown straw, black velvet with bows to outline
the head's crown, blue faille with white felt posies, hats
molded to perfection, all bought for *The Holidays,* new
every year to match a navy crepe suit, to blend with a striped
gabardine sheath, to top a wool coat when October wind
chilled the walk to synagogue. Hats worn once each, never
the next year, *everyone saw this already*, she'd say.

Throw out those sweaters, say my daughters, *clean up*
the house, and why those hats? The sweaters? Sometimes
I hold them close to remind me of my girl with the ghostly
white powder, echoes of arguments between two sisters
who rarely shared. Maybe I'll toss them.   Maybe.

The hats? They stay. When no one sees, I don
them, one at a time, to watch my mother pray.

About the Author

Gail Fishman Gerwin, a Paterson, New Jersey, native, received her bachelor's degree from Goucher College and her master's degree from New York University. In 1984 she founded the Morristown, New Jersey, writing / editing firm *inedit.* Her collection *Sugar and Sand* was a 2010 Paterson Poetry Prize finalist; her second collection *Dear Kinfolk,* (www.chayacairnpress.com) earned a 2013 Paterson Award for Literary Excellence. Gail also authored the plays *Bella's Family* and *Dropping Names,* and the monologue set *Women in Motion.* Her poetry, book reviews, short fiction, essays, and drama appear in print and online literary journals and on stage. She is associate poetry editor of *Tiferet.* She facilitates writing workshops, presents readings, and participates in panels on the creative process. Gail and her husband Kenneth are parents of two daughters and grandparents of three boys and a girl.

Visit Gail's website at: www.gailfgerwin.com

Made in the USA
Lexington, KY
18 December 2015